Grandparents' Day 2014

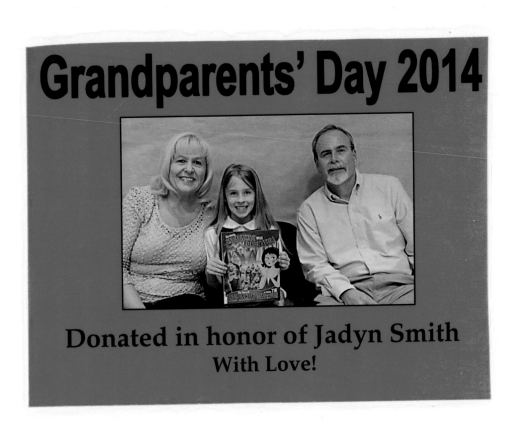

Donated in honor of Jadyn Smith
With Love!

Seriously, SNOW WHITE WAS SO FORGETFUL!

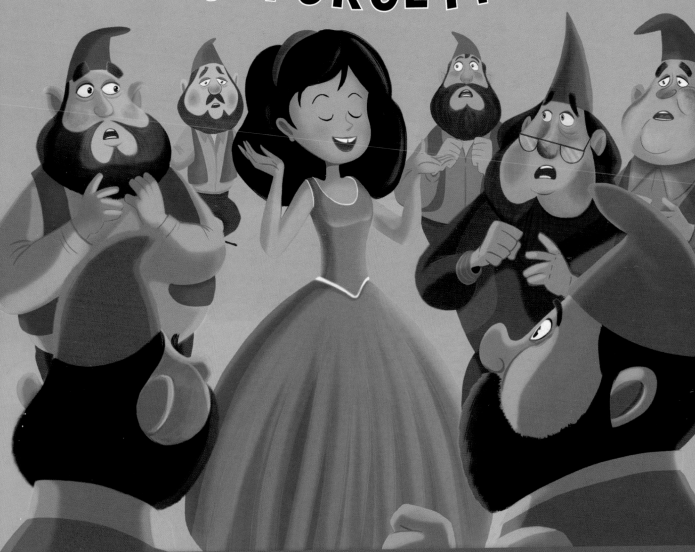

The Story of SNOW WHITE as Told by THE DWARVES

by Nancy Loewen   illustrated by Gerald Guerlais

PICTURE WINDOW BOOKS
a capstone imprint

Special thanks to our adviser, Terry Flaherty, PhD, Professor of English, Minnesota State University, Mankato, for his expertise.

❦

Editor: Jill Kalz
Designer: Lori Bye
Art Director: Nathan Gassman
Production Specialist: Jennifer Walker
The illustrations in this book were created digitally.

❦

Picture Window Books
1710 Roe Crest Drive
North Mankato, MN 56003
www.capstonepub.com

Library of Congress Cataloging-in-Publication Data
Loewen, Nancy, 1964–
Seriously, Snow White was so forgetful! : the story of Snow White as told by the dwarves / by Nancy Loewen ; illustrated by Gerald Guerlais.
p. cm. — (The other side of the story)
ISBN 978-1-4048-7937-9 (library binding) — ISBN 978-1-4048-8085-6 (paperback) — ISBN 978-1-4795-0005-5 (eBook PDF)
[1. Memory—Fiction. 2. Humorous stories.] I. Guerlais, Gerald, ill. II. Title.
PZ7.L837Ser 2013
[E]—dc23

2012029563

Printed in the United States of America in North Mankato, Minnesota.
092012   006933CGS13

I love Snow White dearly. She's a beautiful person, inside and out.

But honestly, the girl's got a mind like a leaky bucket.

Here's the REAL story of Snow White and the Seven Dwarves. (My name, by the way, is Seven. We dwarves used to have real names, but Snow White couldn't remember them.)

3

One day, we came home from the mines to find our cottage door open. We thought we'd been burgled! But no. It was just a lovely little girl, sound asleep.

In the morning she had quite a story to tell.

"Hello!" she said. "I'm Snow White. The queen sent me into the woods, and a hunter was supposed to kill me, but he was nice and let me go, and I wandered a long time in the woods. I guess I'm very pretty, and that's why the queen doesn't like me. I'm Snow White. Would it be all right if I lived with you? I love playing house, and keeping house for real wouldn't be all that different, would it? Did I tell you my name is Snow White?"

Wow, did she have energy.

Life with Snow White was … interesting. She'd forget to turn on the stove. She'd forget to turn it *off.*

She'd make banana cream pie and forget the bananas.

She'd knit scarves that were 10 feet long—just because she forgot to stop.

On the bright side, she laughed at all of our jokes. And she never complained about anything.

Years passed. Snow White grew up, but she didn't really change. She remained her sweet, charming, forgetful self.

Then one day, Five heard a rumor.

"The queen knows Snow White is alive!" he told us.
"The magic mirror spilled the beans!"

We gave Snow White orders to stay inside the cottage. She was not to open the door to anyone. We knew the evil queen would try to hurt her.

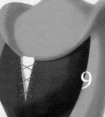

But Snow White quickly forgot.
Twice we came home to find her
lying on the floor. It was clearly
the work of the queen.

The first time,
Snow White couldn't
breathe. She was wearing
a brand-new corset that
was laced too tightly.

The second time she had a poisoned comb in her hair.

All the queen had to do was dress up as an old woman and
offer something pretty for sale. Any thoughts of being
careful went right out of Snow White's head!

10

We posted reminders. We even wrote

DO NOT OPEN THE DOOR

in syrup on her pancakes.

11

But once again we came home to find Snow White on the floor. This time we couldn't help her. There was no corset to loosen or comb to remove. We thought she was dead, killed by a magical spell. And yet, days passed, and she remained as lovely as ever.

"It's like she's forgotten how to wake up," Five whispered.

We couldn't make ourselves bury her. So we placed Snow White in a glass coffin and brought her to a spot on the mountainside. We took turns guarding her.

Thank goodness, that's not the end of the story!

One day I heard voices in the woods.

No, your majesty, it's not time for lunch. We ate our lunch an hour ago. Don't you remember?

Oh, right! Silly me.

Suddenly I was face-to-face with a prince! But he barely noticed me. He couldn't take his eyes off Snow White.

"What happened to her?" he asked. "What's her name?"

I told him the whole story.

"She's the most beautiful girl I've ever seen," he breathed. "Those lips, those eyes! What did you say her name was? Could I take her with me? Now that I've seen her, I don't think I can live without her! What silky hair she has! Tell me again, what's her name?"

I smiled. The prince reminded me of a certain someone.

15

We were bringing Snow White back to the cottage, so the other dwarves could say good-bye. Without warning the prince stopped and turned around. "Hey, what about lunch?" he asked.

The servants slipped.

The coffin slid.

And Snow White coughed.

I'd never heard such a beautiful sound. Out of her throat flew a bit of rosy red apple. Rosy red POISONED apple, that is.

She sat up. **"Did someone say something about lunch?"** she asked.

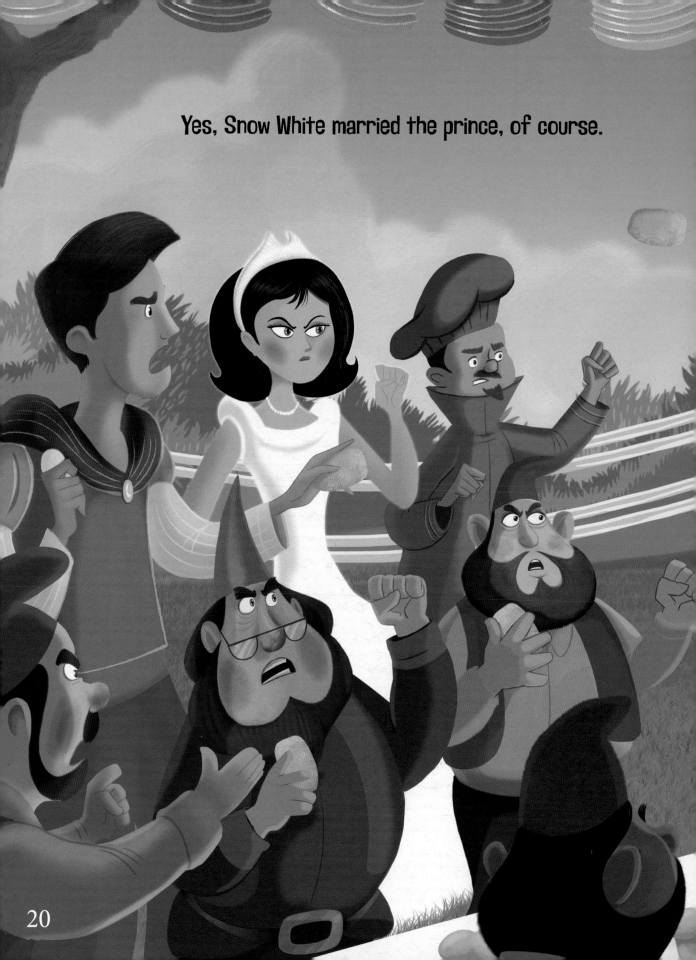

Yes, Snow White married the prince, of course.

The queen actually showed up at the reception, if you can believe it. Everyone threw dinner rolls at her and booed so loudly that she ran away and was never heard from again.

Things are pretty much back to normal now. When it gets cold outside, we're grateful for our 10-foot scarves. And every once in a while, we make banana cream pie without any bananas. Just for old times' sake.

Think About It

Fairy tales have been around a long time and often have many different versions. What version of *Snow White and the Seven Dwarves* do you know best? How is it different from this one? How is it the same?

Who would you rather be friends with: someone who makes a lot of mistakes but is easy to get along with, or someone who does things well but points out all the things you do wrong?

The narrator in this story doesn't have a real name. Would you have felt differently about him if he'd had a name? How about if he were named One, or Four, or any of the other numbers?

How do you think the story would be different if it was told from the queen's point of view? How about the prince's point of view?

⚜

Glossary

narrator—a person who tells a story
point of view—a way of looking at something
version—an account of something from a certain point of view

Read More

Gág, Wanda, trans. and ill. *Snow White and the Seven Dwarfs.* Minneapolis: University of Minnesota Press, 2004.

Powell, Martin, retold by. *Snow White: The Graphic Novel.* Graphic Spin. Mankato, Minn.: Stone Arch Books, 2009.

Santore, Charles, ill. *Snow White: A Tale from the Brothers Grimm.* New York: Sterling, 2010.

Internet Sites

FactHound offers a safe, fun way to find Internet sites related to this book. All of the sites on FactHound have been researched by our staff.

Here's all you do:
Visit *www.facthound.com*
Type in this code: 9781404879379

Look for all the books in the series:

Believe Me, Goldilocks Rocks!
Honestly, Red Riding Hood Was Rotten!
No Lie, I Acted Like a Beast!
Seriously, Cinderella Is SO Annoying!
Seriously, Snow White Was SO Forgetful!
Trust Me, Jack's Beanstalk Stinks!

Super-cool stuff! Check out projects, games and lots more at
www.capstonekids.com